ディ・マウアー
DIE MAUER
The Berlin Wall 1981-1991
GEORGE HASHIGUCHI

ベルリンの壁
1981-1991

橋口譲二

第二次世界大戦の敗戦国・ドイツの首都であったベルリンは、戦後1945年以来、英米仏ソの連合軍による共同管理下に置かれていたが、東から西への人口流出が絶えないため、1961年8月13日、ソ連軍の手により一夜にして東西を隔てる「ベルリンの壁」が築かれた。その後、英米仏の管理区域は西ベルリン、ソ連の管理区域は東ベルリンと呼ばれるようになる。西ベルリンの面積は約480km²、東ベルリンの面積は約400km²、旧東ドイツの真っただ中に位置していた。

西ベルリンを囲む壁は全長約153km、東西ベルリンの間を43km、西ベルリンと東ドイツの境界部分110kmに渡って走っていた。壁の大部分は高さ4m、厚さ15〜30cmのコンクリートでできており、壁に沿っては252か所の監視塔、262か所のシェパード出動待機所が置かれ、1万人以上の東独兵が警備に当たっていた。

西ベルリンと西ドイツをつなぐ交通路の出入口はアウトバーンが2か所、鉄道が2か所、貨物用水路1か所、航空路3か所。東西ベルリン間を行き来できる検問所は7か所。うち外国人が利用できるのはSバーンのフリードリッヒ街駅とチェックポイント・チャーリーの2か所だけだった。道は80か所以上が壁のために分断されていた。

壁に囲まれた西ベルリンは東ドイツに浮かぶ、文字通り「陸の孤島」であった。

Following the defeat of the German Third Reich, its capital Berlin was placed beneath the joint administration of four Allied powers (United States, Britain, France, and the Soviet Union). The population exodus from East to West continued without letup, however, and on August 13 1961 the Soviet Union erected the Berlin Wall overnight, a physical barrier to separate the two sides of the city. Thereafter, the British, U.S., and French sectors of the city came to be known as "West Berlin," while the Soviet sector was called "East Berlin." West Berlin had an area of 480 km^2, and the area of East Berlin was 400 m^2. The city was located in the very center of East Germany.

The wall surrounding West Berlin had a total length of 153 km, including 43 km that divided the west and east halves of the city, and 110 km separating the rest of West Berlin from the surrounding East German countryside. In most places, the wall was a concrete structure four meters high and 15–30 centimeters thick. Some 252 guard towers were situated along the entire length of the wall, together with 262 posts for guard dogs. More than 10,000 East-German soldiers were assigned the job of guarding the wall.

Transportation routes linking West Berlin and East Berlin included two Autobahn (expressway), two railroads, one freight canal and three air routes. Seven checkpoints linked the east and west sides of the city. Of those, the only ones that could be used by foreigners were the Friedrichstrasse Station on the Stadtbahn railway, and The U.S.-administered Checkpoint Charlie. Due to the wall, roads were cut in more than eighty locations. Surrounded by The Wall, West Berlin found itself a "walled island" floating in the middle of East Germany.

プロローグ
1981年12月、僕は初めてベルリンの街角に立った。
ベルリンは空き地が多く、デコボコした街だった。それに街のいたる所に塀があった。
ちょっと走ると道路は行き止まり、塀に会う。
初めはただの塀ぐらいにしか思っていなかったが、それが東西ベルリンを分ける壁だと知った時、
戦慄とも驚きとも言い表わせない何かが僕の体の中を走り、ベルリンの街にいる間じゅう、体が震えて止まらなかった。
僕は壁があまりにも身近にあるのに驚いてしまった。
国境の見えない日本で育ってきた僕には、まず国境が目に見えることが新鮮だった。
西ベルリンは四方を壁で囲まれ、まるで大きな動物園と同じだった。
監視塔の中の警備兵は東からの逃亡者を見張ると同時に必ずこちらを双眼鏡で見ている。
僕らが物見台から東を見るように、彼らも西を見ていた。
しかし僕には、西ベルリンに住む若い人達にとって、壁の存在が時には母親の役割をしているような気がしてならなかった。
道はいたる所で壁に突き当たり、分断されていた。
その結果、街は都市としての本来の機能を失い、大都市でありながら街じゅうに
廃墟や空き地がたくさんあるという、経済効率とはまったく無縁な都市ができあがっていた。
そして都市が機能していないだけに、他の大都市に比べ、干渉されることなくさまざまな実験や試みが繰り返されていた。
それから10年、僕は毎年のようにベルリンに足を運び、街角に立った。
今、壁がなくなった風景の中に立ってみると、今まで僕をベルリンに駆り立てていたのは、
写真家としてベルリンの街を記録したいという思い以上に、陸路や空路に関係なく、
ベルリンの街に入る時に必ず僕の体を支配していた緊張と期待と不安だったような気がしてならない。
ベルリンの街そのものが僕にとって麻薬みたいなものだった。

Prologue
I first set foot in Berlin in December 1981.
The town neighborhoods included numerous areas of open ground,
and street scenes were a series of irregular bumps and depressions.
Walls seemed to appear everywhere one turned.
Driving a short distance on most any road would inevitably bring one to a barrier signaling a dead end.
At first, I thought of the walls as merely an ordinary obstacle,
but when I realized it was The Wall separating East and West Berlin, I felt a strange emotion racing inside,
an inexpressible shudder or start, and I felt like my body was shaking for the rest of my stay in Berlin.
I was startled to find that The Wall was so close. Born and raised in Japan with its invisible borders,
I felt struck by the uniqueness of a national border that could be seen with the eyes.
Surrounded on four sides by The Wall, West Berlin was almost like an immense zoo.
And everywhere one looked there were the watchtowers, their guards on the lookout for persons
trying to escape from the East, while also using their binoculars to watch those of us on the West side.
Just as we could climb observation platforms to look into the East side, they were watching the West as well.
But I had the strong sense that The Wall also served in a kind of mothering role for many of the
young people living in West Berlin. Roads ran into, and were blocked by,
The Wall on every side, with the result that the town had lost its original functions as a city.
While remaining a large urban area, numerous open and abandoned areas could be found here and there,
resulting in the formation of a metropolis totally unrelated to principles of economic efficiency.
And just because the city did not function as other big cities did,
it became host to an unimpeded variety of lifestyles and experimental modes of existence.
For the next ten years, I returned to Berlin each year and stood, watching, on its street corners.
With the reunification of the two Germanies, The Wall has disappeared from Berlin's city scenes.
I now stand on its street corners and cannot help thinking that what drove me back time and time
again was not really the demands of my work as a photographer recording the streets of that city.
No, more than that it was the sensation of tension, expectation and unease
that ruled my emotions each time I arrived in Berlin, whether by land or by air.
I was drawn by Berlin's own narcotic attraction.

ベルリンには森もあれば湖もあった。もちろん、そこにも壁はあった。
ある日、森を抜けて湖のほとりに出ると、ちょうどたそがれ時で湖面が紫色に輝いていた。
静かな風景が目の前に広がっていた。反対側の国境にも等間隔に灯がついた。
横の入江に停まっているヨットにも灯がついた。足元を見ると、小さな石の上にアヒルの親子が寝ている。
手を伸ばせば触れられる所にいるのに、アヒルは逃げようともしない。
静かだった。耳を澄まして、僕はいろんな音を聞いた。いろんな音の中に、対岸の壁の向こうから犬の吠える声が聞こえてくる。
夜になると国境沿いに監視用の軍用犬シェパードが放されるらしい。
しばらくすると、犬の声に混じってドーン、ドーンと空気を震わせる大きな大砲のような音が聞こえてきた。友達が口を開いた。
「5キロ先にソ連の戦車の演習場があるんだ」
「こんな夜なのに？」
「戦争には昼も夜もないよ」
すると今度は僕らの後ろのほうから、ドーン、ドーンと同じような音がする。
アメリカ軍だという。僕は突然身震いを感じた。

Berlin encompasses both forests and lakes. And, of course, The Wall went there, too.
One day, I passed through a woods and stood on the bank of a lake just as twilight was dyeing
the lake with a veneer of deep purple. A scene of peace unfolded before my eyes.
Along the border on the opposite side, electric lights were burning at equidistant intervals,
and lights also illumined a sailboat moored at the lake's inlet.
Looking down at my feet, I saw a family of ducks lying quietly on a bed of small rocks.
They were so close I could have reached out and touched them,
but the ducks did not appear afraid, and remained without running away.
It was most quiet. Training my ears, I could hear a variety of sound.
Among all the sounds, I could hear a barking of dogs from the far side of The Wall on the opposite shore.
It was evening, and they were probably letting loose the military patrol dogs along the border.
After a short time, I heard mixed with the dog's voices a deep thumping sound
that caused the air to quake like the reverberation of a cannon.
I asked my friend about the sound.
He said, "About five kilometers over there is a firing range for Soviet tanks."
I was surprised. "Even at this time of night?"
"There's no day or night in war."
In a few minutes more, I began hearing the same thumping sound behind us, on our side of the border.
My friend said this time it was the Americans. My body suddenly shivered.

友達と、彼が生まれ育った村を見に行ったことがある。友達の生まれた村は壁の向こう側、東ベルリンの郊外にあった。
彼は壁が築かれたその夜、友人と二人で西ベルリンに逃げて来た。
車は国境である運河沿いに走り出した。牧草地が見え隠れし、風景の中に牛が目につき始めていた。
中心街クーダムから30分もたっていないのに、心休まる風景だった。運河の向こう岸には
背の高い月見草が群生している。黄色い花が赤みがかった夕方の鈍い光の中で風に揺れていた。
突然、月見草の花の中にカーキ色の服を着た男達が4人現われた。
4人とも肩に自動小銃を担ぎ、胸には双眼鏡をかけている。一人は無線機を担いでいる。
「東のパトロールだよ」
友達がそう言いながら車のスピードを緩めると、その4人は足を止め、双眼鏡で僕らのほうを見た。
車を止めて外に出ると、パトロール隊と僕らの間に視界をさえぎるものは何もなく、
足元に10メートル幅の運河が流れているだけだった。パトロール隊の中には、見るからに若く
顔じゅうニキビだらけの少年が一人いた。4人とも表情一つ変えずに僕らのほうを凝視している。
「彼らに許されている自由といえば、何かがあった時に銃を撃つか、立ち小便をするぐらいなんだよ」
と友達が言った。彼らに対して友達がただ単に否定的な言葉を吐いただけかのように聞こえたが、
僕はその言葉の裏に、否応なしに一つの運命を互いに共有し合っている者同士の、いつくしみと嘆きと人間愛を感じた。

I went with a friend to see the village where he had been born and raised.
The village lay on the other side of The Wall, on the outskirts of East Berlin.
But on the night The Wall was built, he had escaped to the West with another friend.
The car ran alongside the canal forming the national border.
Pastures were visible here and there, and in their midst we began to see an occasional cow.
Although we hadn't come more than thirty minutes from the main streets of central Berlin,
we already found ourselves within a tranquil pastoral landscape.
On the other bank of the canal grew bushes of wild primroses.
Tinted red by the dull light of evening, the yellow flowers were swaying in the wind.
Suddenly, four men dressed in khaki appeared from behind the primroses.
Each of the four carried a submachine gun on his shoulder,
and had binoculars resting against his chest. One carried a radio transmitter.
"It's one of the East's patrols."
While speaking, my friend slowed the car.
The four men stopped and viewed us through their binoculars.
When we stopped the car and got out, there was nothing to block the line of sight,
and only the ten-meter-wide canal flowing at our feet lay between us.
One of the members of the patrol appeared very young, his face full of pimples.
The four men continued to stare at us with changeless expressions.
My friend said, "You know how much freedom they're allowed? When something happens,
they get to decide whether to shoot their guns or take a piss."
It appeared that my friend had merely spit the malicious words at the other men,
but behind his comment, I felt the affection, sorrow,
and humanitarian fellow-feeling of men impartially sharing a common fate.

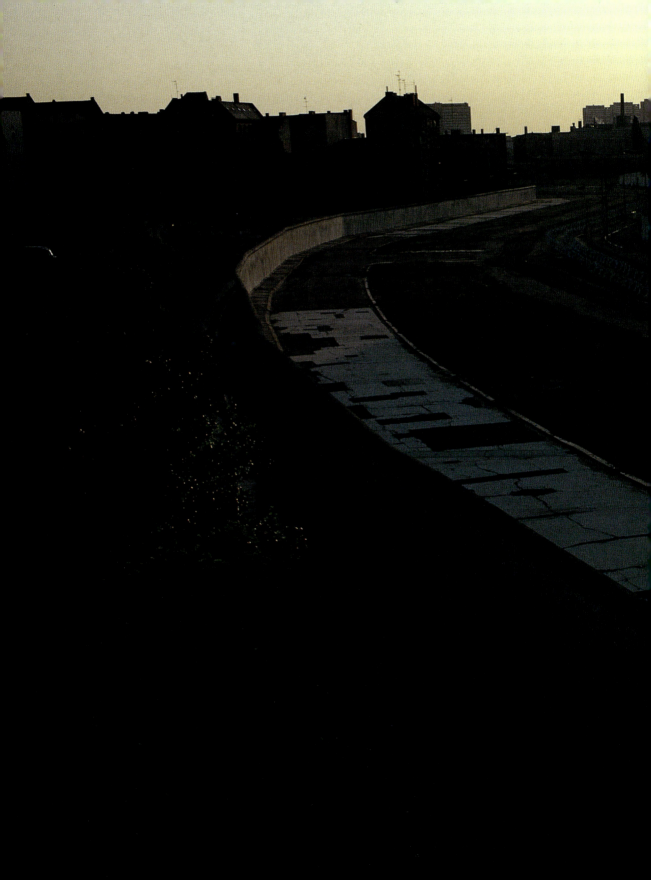

壁が崩壊してからというもの、僕は何度となく壁をはさんで東西ベルリンを行ったり来たりした。
ある日、西ベルリンの南端、グロピウス・シュタット地区の近くを走っている壁を越えて東に入った。
その日はとても寒く、目に映るものすべてが凍り始めていた。足元の土もコチコチに凍っていた。
以前壁が崩壊する前、物見台から見た時、今僕が立っている場所には、辺り一面麦畑が広がっていた。
その麦も今は刈り取られ、切り株は掘り返されて黒い土だけの畑が広がっていた。
靴のつま先で凍りついた土を蹴飛ばしてみたが、固くて崩れない。逆に僕の足のほうが痛くなってきた。
恐らく春が来るまではこのままなんだろうと思った。
壁越しに、さまざまな生活音が聞こえてきた。
車のブレーキの音、子供のはしゃぐ声、教会の鐘の音、時を告げる学校のチャイムの音。
今度は意識して壁に背を向け、東のほうに目をやってみた。そこには畑が広がり、畑の横、
僕のすぐ斜め前には小さな集落があった。集落からは音一つ聞こえてこない。
時々ニワトリの鳴き声と犬の鳴き声が聞こえてくるくらいだった。
ここの村の人達は壁があった30年もの間、壁越しに聞こえてくる、
自分たちの生活とはまったく関係のない生活音を一体どんな思いで耳にしてきたんだろうか。
そう思うと、突然僕の中に熱いものがこみ上げてきた。

Since The Wall was removed in 1989,
I have traveled numerous times between East and West Berlin.
One day, I crossed The Wall near the Gropiusstadt area and entered East Berlin.
The day was very cold, and everything I saw was beginning to freeze.
The ground was frosty, crunching beneath my feet. Before The Wall was destroyed,
I could look into the East from the observation platform and see the place I now stood;
It had been covered in barley fields. The barley had now been harvested, however,
and the stubble had been plowed under, leaving nothing but broad fields of black earth.
I tried kicking a frozen clod with the tip of my shoe, but it held solid and couldn't be budged;
on the contrary, my toe began hurting.
"It'll probably stay this way until the coming of spring," I thought.
When I passed The Wall, I was gradually able to hear a variety of the sounds of life.
The screech of automobile brakes,
voices of children at play, church bells, chimes from a school clock signaling the hour.
Deliberately turning my back to The Wall, I focused my eyes toward the East.
Fields spread out before me and beside them lay a small community,
oriented at a slight diagonal from my front. But I could hear no sounds from the settlement.
Only the occasional cry of a rooster or the barking of a dog.
The people of this village had lived for the past thirty years,
hearing sounds of life coming from beyond The Wall, sounds totally unrelated to their own lives.
I wondered now what they had thought, what they had felt when they had listened to those sounds.
And with that reflection, I felt hot tears suddenly welling up from inside.

壁が崩壊した1か月後、東ベルリンに住む一人の青年と、西ベルリン・クロイツベルグのクナイペで知り合いになった。
彼は壁ができた年、つまり1961年生まれの28歳、病院で働いていた。
彼は壁が崩壊した2日後の11月11日、生まれて初めて西ベルリンに足を踏み入れた。
「特別な時に飲もうと思って取っておいたケンタッキーっていう名のウイスキーを、壁を通った後に1本飲んだ。
壁を渡ったのはベルナウアー通りに新しく壊された場所。そこから西に出て物見台に立ち、
西側から東側を眺めてみた。本当は知っている道のはずなのに、まったく違う風景に見えた。
それからスーパーマーケットに行って新聞『ベルリナー・モルゲン・ポスト』をタダでもらって、バナナを4本買った。
そのあと地下鉄でクロイツベルグへ行き、フリードリッヒ街駅で友達に会い、子供のおもちゃ屋に行った。
壁に沿ってチェックポイント・チャーリーまで歩いて行き、博物館に入った。
ブランデンブルグ門、ライヒスタークを見て、映画『ベルリン・天使の詩』を見た。
それから地下鉄に乗ろうとしたけど人が多過ぎて乗れなかったから、クーダムまで歩いた。
10時間西ベルリンにいて、それで十分だと思った。
東ベルリンに戻ってから、フリードリッヒ街駅の近くのレストランに入り、
シャンパンを飲んで小さなステーキを食べたよ。食べ終わってからやっぱりこれは夢じゃないか、と思った」

About one month after The Wall was opened in late 1989,
I was at a pub in the Kreuzberg section of West Berlin, where I met a young man from the East.
A hospital worker, he was twenty-eight years old,
born in 1961 — the same year The Wall had been erected.
He set foot in West Berlin for the first time on November 11 1989,
two days after The Wall was breached. He told me the following:
"I had a bottle of whiskey called Kentucky that I'd been saving for a special occasion.
I drank the entire bottle after passing through The Wall.
I came across at a newly opened spot on Bernauer Street.
From there I went to the observation platforms and looked at the East from the West.
It looked completely different, even though I must have known what all the streets were.
From there, I went to a supermarket and they gave me a free copy of the Berliner Morgen Post;
I also bought four bananas. Then I took the subway to Kreuzberg
and met a friend at Friedrichstrasse Station, and went to a toy store.
I walked along The Wall until I got to Checkpoint Charlie; then I went into a museum.
I saw the Brandenburg Gate, the Reichstag, and watched the movie "Der Himmel über Berlin."
I was going to ride the subway again, but there were too many people, so I couldn't get on.
Instead, I walked as far as Kurfürstendamm.
I had been in West Berlin for ten hours, and I thought that was enough.
After returning to East Berlin, I went into a restaurant not far from Friedrichstrasse Station
and had a small steak and drank Champagne.
When I finished eating, I wondered if it weren't, indeed, all a dream."

ある日、乗り合わせたタクシーの運転手が言った。
「この街は文化の母体なんだ。この街は母親みたいに文化を生んで見守り、育てる。それがベルリンだよ」
僕が西ベルリンに行く楽しみの一つに、壁の絵を見に行くということがあった。
壁の絵は、行くたびに増え、新しく変わっていた。
おもしろいのは、誰が認めるわけでもないのにいい絵は残り、
下手だと思う絵は必ず消えて、またその上に新しい絵が描かれていることだった。
中には描かれた絵の横に作者の名前と電話番号が記してあるのもあった。
壁は人の流れを断ち切った代わりに、ベルリンの街に白いキャンバスを用意してくれていた。

One day, I took a taxi and the driver spoke to me:
"This town is the womb of culture. This town gives birth to culture
and nurtures it, just like a mother. That is Berlin."
One of my pleasures in visiting West Berlin
was the expectation of seeing the graffiti drawings on The Wall.
The pictures seemed to change and grow in number each time I visited Berlin.
Although there was no official judge of the artistic merit of these picutres,
I was struck by the fact that the good pictures would invariably remain,
while the poorer ones would disappear and be painted over by others.
Some pictures even included the names and telephone numbers of their artists.
As thought in return for cutting off the flow of humanity,
The Wall provided those who remained with a new, white canvas for their expression.

壁が崩壊した後、僕の友達はいつも苛立っていた。日曜日の朝カフェで一緒に共有し合うような、
ゆったりとした時間軸の中に身を置いていても、心の隅でイライラしていることに変わりはなかった。
彼女は東ベルリンからの亡命者だった。ところが東西ドイツが統合され、
とりあえずすべての東ドイツ市民が「自由」を手に入れることができるようになった今、
「亡命者」という言葉は意味を持たなくなった。
「この1年はしょっちゅう怒りを感じてたわ。それはある限られたDDR（東ドイツ）の人たちに対する怒り……
彼らは長い間DDRに残り、国家の言うことをよく聞いて仕えてきたのに、
革命を起こしたのは自分たちだって言うの。
この1年間は壁がなくなって嬉しかったけど、一方では悲しかったわ。
それは今、こんなに簡単になったことへの代償を、私自身が払わなければならなかったから。
今ではまったく当たり前になったことのために、私は恋人を失い、家族を失い、安定を失い、投獄されたの。
私はただ、東ベルリンから西ベルリンに行きたかっただけなのに……」
彼女と一緒にいると、彼女の後ろのほうで同じようにさまよい始めている、かつての亡命者たちの姿が目に浮かんでくる。
壁の向こう側から逃れて来た人々が、壁がなくなった今、見えない壁や自由に縛られ始めている。
むごい現実の中に、僕の友達はいた。
この冬、大雪が降った日の翌日、僕は他の友達3人とヘリコプターをチャーターしてベルリンの街を空から見ていた。
壁に沿い、150メートルの低空飛行で飛んでもらったはずなのに、
よほどしっかり見ていない限り壁の跡はわからなかった。
それに空から見ると、壁の跡地のなんと狭かったことか。
僕は空の上で思わずつぶやいていた。
「たったこれだけの幅だったのか……」

After the destruction of The Wall, my friend was constantly annoyed.
Even though she superficially placed herself in the same relaxed time frame that she might share
during a Sunday-morning coffee, some corner of her mind remained troubled.
She had fled from East Germany, seeking asylum. But with the reunification of East and West,
all the former citizens of the East had automatically received "freedom", and the term
"political asylum" had lost its former meaning.
"I've felt mad a lot this past year. I've been particularly mad at certain people in the DDR (East Germany) . . . . .
They stayed behind for so long in the East, doing everything the government said,
and being good servants, but now they're claiming that they're the ones that started the revolution.
I was glad The Wall disappeared this last year, but at the same time, I was sad, too.
I had to pay a high price for something that they all now get for free.
To get the freedom they now take for granted, I had to give up my boyfriend, my family, my stability —
I was even thrown in jail. And just because I wanted to go from East Berlin to the West . . ."
While with this woman, I began to see somewhere behind her the figures of all those earlier refugees,
who in the same way are now beginning to wander restlessly.
The people who fled from the other side of The Wall are now being shackled by another,
invisible wall, and by their own freedom. My friend was caught inside a cruel reality.
This winter, the day after a major snowfall, I chartered a helicopter with three other friends
and viewed the city of Berlin from the air. I asked the pilot to fly 150 meters above the ground
along The Wall, but even at that low altitude it was almost impossible, without great concentration,
to make out where The Wall had been. And when viewed from the sky, it became apparent
that the space occupied by The Wall was even narrower than I had thought.
I suddenly began sobbing into the winter sky. "For something only this wide . . ."

1989年、ライプツィヒで高まった東ドイツ国内の民主化要求の波はまたたく間に東ドイツ全土に広がった。その夏、オーストリア・ハンガリー国境が開放されるやいなや、大量の東ドイツ国民が第三国を経由して国外へ亡命、ホーネッカー議長による独裁体制が崩壊した。
そして1989年11月9日、ついにベルリンの壁は崩壊した。
西への東独人大量脱出、それに伴う社会の機能麻痺は、東西ドイツの再統一の声を浮上させ、1990年7月1日、通貨統合によって東ドイツ・マルクは消滅、1990年10月3日、東西ドイツは再統一され、東ドイツは地図上から姿を消した。
そして1991年6月20日、ベルリンは統一ドイツの首都と決定された。

The democratization movement that began in the East German city of Leipzig in 1989 soon spread throughout the entire country of East Germany. During the summer of that year, borders were opened with Austria and Hungary, and massive numbers of East Germans fled to the West through third countries, signaling the collapse of the regime of General Secretary Erich Honecker. On November 9 1989 the Berlin Wall finally crumbled.
The sudden influx of easterners to the West and the accompanying paralysis of social services and functions led to cries for reunion of the two Germanies. The unification of currencies on July 1 1990 eliminated the East-German Deutschemark, and on October 3 1990 East Germany and West Germany were formally reunited: East Germany disappeared from the map.
Finally, on June 20 1991 a new capital was selected for reunited Germany. The choice went to Berlin.

DATA

1989.12 西：ベタニエン通り ①
Bethanien Str, West

1989.12 西：ベタニエン通り ②
Bethanien Str, West

1989.12 東：グロツィエッテンから見た西のアパート群 ③
Western skyscraper, Großziethen District, East

1983.5 西：ポツダム広場 ④
Potsdamer Square, West

1991.1 西：オーバーバウム橋から見たシュプレー川 ⑤
Spree River from the Oberbaum Bridge, West

1989.12 西：ゲーリッツ駅跡地 ⑥
Ex Görlitzer Station, West

1989.12 東：エルゼン通り ⑦
Elsen Str, West

1984.2 西：オーバーバウム橋から見たシュプレー川 ⑧
Spree River from the Oberbaum Bridge, West

1983.7 西：ヴァンゼー ⑨
Wannsee District, West

1983.7 西：ヴァンゼー ⑩
Wannsee District, West

1983.6 西：ポツダム広場 ⑪
Potsdamer Square, West

1990.1 東：エバースヴァルド通り ⑫
Eberswalder Str, East

1983.6 西：リュバース ⑬
Lübars District, West

1983.7 西：Sバーン，フリードリッヒ街駅と ⑭
レーター駅間の監視用地帯
Death Stripe between S-bahn Friedrichstr Station
and Lehrter Station, West

1983.6 西：リュバース ⑮
Lübars District, West

1981.11 西：グロピウス・シュタット地区 ⑯
Gropiusstadt, West

1983.7 西：シュプレー川 ⑰
Spree River, West

1984.4 西：ケープニック通り沿いのシュプレー川 ⑱
Spree River along Köpnicker Str, West

1983.5 西：ライヒスターク裏のシュプレー川 ⑲
Spree River flowing behind the Reichstag, West

1984.7 西：オーバーバウム橋 ⑳
Oberbaum Bridge, West

1983.7 西：聖トーマス教会 ㉑
St.Thomas Church, West

1983.7 西：聖トーマス教会 ㉒
St.Thomas Church, West

1983.6 西：ストレセマン通り ㉓
Stresemann Str, West

1990.9 東：インヴァリデン墓地内の ㉔
監視塔から見た西
A view of West Berlin from the
watchtower in Invaliden Cemetery

1989.12 東：エルゼン通り ㉕
Elsen Str, East

1989.12 西：ヴァルダマー通り ㉖
Waldemar Str, West

1989.12 東：ベルナウアー通り ㉗
Bernauer Str, East

1983.7 西：エバート通り ㉘
Ebert Str, West

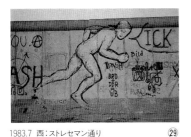

1983.7 西：ストレセマン通り ㉙
Stresemann Str, West

1983.7 西：ストレセマン通り ㉚
Stresemann Str, West

1983.7 西：ストレセマン通り ㉛
Stresemann Str, West

1989.12 東：ベルナウアー通り ㉜
Bernauer Str, East

1989.12 東：ベルナウアー通り ㉝
Bernauer Str, East

1989.12 東：ベルナウアー通り ㉞
Bernauer Str, East

1984.7 西：ストレセマン通り ㉟
Stresemann Str, West

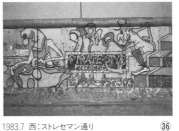

1983.7 西：ストレセマン通り ㊱
Stresemann Str, West

1984.7 西：ストレセマン通り ㊲
Stresemann Str, West

1984.2 西：アンハルター駅廃墟 ㊳
Ruins of Anhalter Station, West

1984.2 西：アンハルター駅廃墟 ㊴
Ruins of Anhalter Station, West

1989.12 東：ベルナウアー通り ㊵
Bernauer Str, East

1990.1 西:トレプトウ橋上に建てられたオブジェ ㊶
『自由の鳥は壁を越えて飛んでいく』
An object titled "Free Bird Fly Over The Wall",
Treptower Bridge, West

1983.7 西:リンデン通り ㊷
Linden Str, West

1989.12 西:リンデン通り ㊸
Linden Str, West

1989.12 西:ストレセマン通り ㊹
Stresemann Str, West

1984.3 西:ツィマー通り ㊺
Zimmer Str, West

1989.12 西:ベタニエン通り ㊻
Bethanien Str, West

1984.3 西:ツィマー通り ㊼
Zimmer Str, West

1990.9 西:ブロミー通り近くのシュプレー川 ㊽
Spree River near Brommy Str, West

1989.12 西:ヴァルダマー通り ㊾
Waldemar Str, West

1984.4 西:シュレジア橋 ㊿
Schlesische Bridge, West

1983.7 西:ライヒスターク裏に立てられた墓碑、㊿
エバート通り
An epitaph built behind the Reichstag, Ebert Str,
West

1989.12 西:ブランデンブルグ門 ㊿
The Brandenburger Gate, West

1989.12.23 東:ブランデンブルグ門開放 ㊿
Opening of the Brandenburger Gate, West

1990.10.3 東:東西ドイツ再統一、ブランデンブルグ門 ㊿
Reunion of the two Germanies,
The Brandenburger Gate, West

エピローグ
予感するものはあった。何かが動き始めているという気配を僕は体の奥のほうで感じていた。
感じていた、といっても、壁が崩れるなんてことは考えもしなかった。壁があるからこそ平和が保たれていると思っていたし、壁が壊れる時は戦争が始まる時だ、と僕は思っていた。そのことはベルリンで暮らしている人たちもちろんのこと、ヨーロッパ大陸における政治状況に興味を持っている人たちの大半が共通認識として同じような考えを持っていたのではないだろうか。
'89年夏から秋にかけての数か月間、僕はロンドンに滞在していた。滞在先の居間に置かれたテレビにある日、ハンガリーの国境を越えて西側に亡命してゆく東ドイツ人の映像が映し出されていた。その日を境に、BBC放送は連日、ハンガリー・オーストリアの国境線の映像をトップニュースで伝え始めた。暗闇を映し出したブラウン管の中からは、荒々しい低く押し殺した息づかいだけが地を這うような感じで聞こえてくる。いくつかの黒い影は用心深く、けれど大胆に暗闇の中を移動していた。まるで映画のワンシーンを見ているようなリアルな映像だった。
その頃まず、ロンドンからベルリンに向かうべきかどうかという、一度目の迷いが僕の中に生まれた。
「普段特にジャーナリスティックな活動をしているわけではないのに、バタバタ出かけて行ってどうなる」
「だけど何かが起こり始めているのは確かだから、立ち会ってみたいし……」
1時間おきに僕の気持はくるくる変化していた。ただ不思議だったのは、亡命者がうごめいているのはハンガリーの国境なのに、行くとしたらベルリンだ、と強く思っている自分の姿があることだった。
結論として、僕はとりあえず帰国することを選んだ。帰国して態勢を整えたのちに、ベルリンに出かけようと思った。
9月末に帰国すると同時に、東ドイツ大使館に取材ビザの申請を出した。ビザ申請の趣旨は、この年の12月から1月にかけて、ベルリンの壁を東ベルリン側から大型カメラで撮りたい、という内容のものだった。ビザ申請の手続きをしている間にも、何万人もの東ドイツ人が、ハンガリーやオーストリアを経由したり、プラハの西ドイツ大使館に逃げ込んだりしていた。
状況は刻一刻変化していた。時代が動き始めていた。かといって時代の大きなうねりが壁を突き破るなんて、この段階ですら僕は想像しえなかった。むしろこの大きなうねりに対して、いつ銃口が向けられるのか、そのことのほうが心配だった。
ビザ申請の手続きが終わると同時に、僕はその頃進めていた作品作りのために、撮影旅行に出かけた。その作品は90年5月、『FATHER』という写真集にまとめ、すでに発表済みである。
ビザ申請をした1週間後の11月9日、僕は岐阜県白川村にいた。そして、小さな郵便局の休憩室に置いてあるテレビで初めて、壁崩壊のニュースを知った。
その瞬間何を思い、何を考えていたのか、僕はよく覚えていない。ただ、息するのを忘れていたことは事実だった。

ブラウン管に映し出された映像を見ながら、「信じられない」「これはウソだ」と思いながらも、「これは現実なんだ」「夢じゃないんだ」と認識するまでに、大して時間は必要なかった。写真家としてベルリンの街を10年間見続けてきたという自負があるだけに、正直なところ、壁崩壊のニュースを見ながら、平和と自由を喜ぶ気持があるのと同時に、間に合わなかったという焦燥感と、その場に偶然居合わせたジャーナリストに対するジェラシーが心の中にあったことも事実だった。
テレビを含めたいくつかのジャーナリズムから、すぐにでもベルリンに飛んで欲しいという要請が、白川村にいる僕に対してあった。結局小さな迷いはあったにせよ、僕はそれらを断わり、郵便局でお茶をごちそうになったあとそのまま予定通り「FATHER」探しの旅を続けた。
89年12月、クリスマスのイルミネーションに包まれたベルリンの街に、すでに大した意味を持たなくなった東ドイツ政府発行の取材ビザを手にして、僕はいた。
街は人で溢れていた。壁崩壊前までは、ブランデンブルグ門やポツダム広場、チェックポイント・チャーリーといった代表的な名所ですら、時々観光バスが来るぐらいで閑散としていたのに、今回は観光ポイントに関係なく、人が溢れていた。
人の流れに視線を送りながら、僕はいろんなことを考え始めていた。
壁の存在が語られる時、東側で暮らす人々の不自由さがよくニュースになるが、壁の存在が、同じように29年間壁に閉ざされてきた西ベルリンの人々にとってどのような影を落としてきたのか、まず語られることは少ない。壁が崩壊した今、初めて西ベルリーナを取り囲む光と影があぶり出されてきたように僕には思えた。
それにしても「壁」っていったい何だったんだろうか？ 国境にしろベルリンの壁にしろ、国家にとってのアイデンティティーであって、個人の存在とはまったく関係ないところで成り立っていた。その関係ない「壁」が個人の行動や生活を支配してきた現実を見ていると、とてもやるせないものを感じる。壁を挟んでどちら側にいたかなんて、まったくの偶然であって、個人の責任でも何でもなかった。かといって、国の責任でもないように思う。あえて責任の元を探すとしたら、人間の存在そのものに責任があるのかもしれない。
壁が崩壊し、東西ドイツが統一してとりあえず人々が自由に行き来できるようになった。旧東ドイツの人たちは、西の人々の生活に触れることで自分たちが置かれている位置を知ることができた。その結果、生活レベルと人間の尊厳は関係ないにもかかわらず、その格差が旧東ドイツの人々の中に卑屈さを生み、心の中に壁を築き始めている。ここにまた、新しい壁が生まれた。目で見える形で存在していた東西を仕切る壁と異なり、心の中の壁は見えない。それだけにもっと始末に悪いような気がする。
僕は、人間社会が存在し続ける限り、「壁」はなくならないと思う。そのことは、国にとっても個人にとっても、同じだと思う。
かといって人間をやめるわけにはいかない。僕らはずっと「壁」と向かい合って生きていかなければならないのかもしれない。

Epilogue

I had a premonition. I felt somewhere deep inside the sensation that something was beginning to move.

But while I felt it, I couldn't imagine that The Wall itself would crumble and disappear. I thought it was only because of The Wall that peace had been maintained, and I assumed that war would begin the moment The Wall disappeared. And wasn't that the usual perception, not only among the people living in Berlin, of course, but among most Europeans? Surely it must have been a common thought among the majority of people who maintained an interest in politics.

I was staying in London during the months between the summer and fall of 1989. One day, the television in the room where I was staying showed images of East Germans fleeing over the Hungarian border to the West. From that day on, the BBC began transmitting images of the Hungarian and Austrian border situation as its top news story. From the dark images of night broadcast through the television tube, one could hear only the rough and stertorous, but forcibly subdued, sounds of breathing, as though the sounds themselves were crawling tightly pressed against the ground. Within several of the black shadows, one could make out images of movement in the dark, some careful, some defiant. It was almost as though we were watching scenes from a movie.

It was then that I experienced my first doubt; a questioning as to whether I shouldn't go from London to Berlin. About once an hour I engaged in the following kind of internal debate:

"You don't normally spend your time as a photo-journalist, so why go flying off the handle just for this?"

"Yes, but it's certain that something is happening, and I want to be there to see it . . ."

What I now consider particularly strange is the fact that while it was the Hungarian border that was then active with asylum-seekers, my first and only intuition was to proceed to Berlin. But as it turned out, I decided instead to return first to Japan. I decided I would go back and set up a systematic plan of action, after which I could go back to the divided city.

When I returned to Japan at the end of September, I simultaneously applied to the East German consulate for a press visa. In my application I said I wanted to spend December and January on the eastern side, photographing The Wall with a large-format camera. But even while I was applying for the visa, several tens of thousands of East Germans were escaping to the West across the Hungarian and Austrian borders, or seeking asylum with the West German embassy in Prague.

Events were evolving with each passing second. The spirit of the age was stirring. I felt it, yet I still could not guess that the ocean swell of this moment would sweep The Wall away in its entirety. On the contrary, I was more worried about the possibility that guns might be trained on the disorder at any moment.

Once my visa application was complete, I set off on a trip inside Japan to complete another photographic project that was already underway. I published the photographs resulting from that journey in the volume "Father" (May, 1990).

On November 9, just one week after making my visa application, I was in the village of Shirakawa, in Japan's Gifu prefecture. Sitting in the waiting room of the village's little post office that day, I was watching the television news when I learned that The Wall had crumbled.

I don't remember now very well what I thought or felt at that instant. I do know, though, that I forgot to breathe. While watching the images on the television screen, I told myself "This can't be real," and "I can't believe it," but it still didn't take me long to realize, "This is really happening — it isn't just a dream."

As a photographer, I had taken it upon myself to record the Berlin Wall for some ten years now, and I watched the scenes of the breaching of The Wall with joy for the new-found sense of peace and freedom signified by the event. But to be honest, I must admit that mixed with that joy I also felt irritation that I had not been there for the event, coupled to professional jealousy toward the journalists who had experienced the happy fortune of being in Berlin merely by chance.

While in Shirakawa Village, I received requests from several television stations and other news organizations, asking me to fly to Berlin immediately and cover the events there. Although I naturally experienced a few misgivings, I refused the offers. After having my tea in Shirakawa's post office, I kept to my plan and went on my way in search of "Father."

December 1989. Holding the press visa issued by the East German government — already a virtually meaningless piece of paper — I stood beside The Wall, bathed with it in Christmas illumination.

Crowds of people swarmed over the city. Until the destruction of The Wall, even such typical tourist attractions as the Brandenburg Gate, Potsdamer Platz, and Checkpoint Charlie were largely abandoned except for the occasional sightseeing bus. But now, people were everywhere, tourist attraction or not.

While passing my eyes over the flow of humanity, I began thinking about a lot of things. When people speak of the existence of The Wall, they most often talk about the lack of freedom experienced by those living on the east side. But they rarely speak about what kind of shadows dropped over the lives of West-Berliners who found themselves likewise hemmed in for some twenty-nine years by the existence of that same wall. It seemed to me that only now, with the passing of The Wall, could we see the developing images of light and shadows that have for so long enveloped the West Berliner.

But then, just what are walls to begin with? Whether a national border or The Berlin Wall, walls originally came into existence only for the identity of the nation, and they had no relation whatsoever to the existence of the individual. And I can't help feeling a terrible sense of gloom when I see the reality, namely, that the movements and lifestyles of so many individuals have been ruled by the totally unrelated existence of The Wall.

What side of the wall one was on, what side one found oneself on — these were matters of sheer chance, pure and simple, and were not the responsibility of any of the individuals thus surrounded. But then, when I ask myself, whose responsibility is it?, I can't say that it is solely the responsibility of the state. I suppose if I were to look for the source of the responsibility, I might have to find it in human existence itself.

With the disappearance of The Wall, and the reunification of East and West Germany, people can once again come and go freely. People from the former country of East Germany have now seen the lives of those living in the West and thus come to know the status in which they themselves have been placed.

And as a result, even though no inherent relation exists between levels of lifestyle and human prestige, that difference in material abundance seems to have given birth to a sense of meanness among the former citizens of East Germany, resulting in the erection of a new wall, the one in their hearts. In contrast to the old, visible wall dividing East and West, the wall in the heart cannot be seen with the eyes, and just for that reason, it may be the harder one to remove.

The Wall will exist so long as human society endures. That holds the same for nations as it does for the hearts of individuals. So long as we cannot cease from the conditions of our humanity, it may be, for that reason alone, that we find ourselves forever condemned to face the impassive existence of The Wall.

Photo by Nils Heineman

橋口譲二 (はしぐちじょうじ)
1949年 鹿児島県生まれ

著書
1982年：写真集「俺たちどこにもいられない」(草思社)
1983年：単行本「いま世界の十代は」(小学館)
1985年：写真集「ここにいたっていいじゃないか」(集英社)
　　　　単行本「ベルリン物語」(情報センター出版局)
1986年：単行本「ソウルの大観覧車」(山口文憲共著、平凡社)
1987年：単行本「まゆみさん物語」(情報センター出版局)
1988年：写真集「十七歳の地図」(文藝春秋)
　　　　単行本・写真集2冊組「南からの風」(扶桑社)
1989年：写真集「動物園」(情報センター出版局)
　　　　単行本「それぞれの時」(草思社)
1990年：写真集「FATHER」(文藝春秋)

受賞
1981年：第18回太陽賞受賞

個展
1983年：「視線」(東京、大阪)
1985年：「ベルリン・囲いの中から」(東京、大阪、名古屋)
1988年：「十七歳」(東京、宮崎、長崎)
1989年：「南からの風」(東京)
　　　　「十七歳」(アルル国際写真展正式招待、パリ)
1990年：「動物園」(東京、名古屋、札幌、大分、所沢)
　　　　「FATHER」(東京、北海道東川町)
　　　　「十七歳」(ローマ)
1991年：「十七歳」(北海道東川町)

HASHIGUCHI George
Born in 1949, Kagoshima, Japan

Books previously completed:
1982　"No place for us to live"(Soshisha)
1983　"Teenagers in the World"(Shogakukan)
1985　"Why can not we stay here?"(Shueisha)
　　　"Berlin Story"(Joho Center Shuppan-kyoku)
1986　"Seoul"(Heibonsha)
1987　"Message to Young People"(Joho Center Shuppan-kyoku)
1988　"Seventeen's Map"(Bungeishunju)
　　　"South Winds"(Fusosha)
1989　"Zoo"(Joho Center Shuppan-kyoku)
　　　"Singles in Tokyo"(Soshisha)
1990　"Father"(Bungeishunju)

Awards:
1981　The 18th TAIYO-Award

Exhibition:
1983　"Gaze"(Tokyo, Osaka)
1985　"Berlin: From the Fence"(Tokyo, Osaka)
1988　"Seventeen"(Tokyo, Nagasaki, Miyazaki)
1989　"South Winds"(Tokyo)
　　　"Avoir 17ans au Japon"(Arles, Paris)
1990　"Zoo"(Tokyo, Nagoya, Sapporo, Oita, Tokorozawa)
　　　"Father"(Tokyo, Higashikawa)
　　　"Seventeen"(Rome)
1991　"Seventeen"(Higashikawa)

Art Director
大島孝雄 OSHIMA Takao
Printing Director
森谷忠義 MORIYA Tadayoshi
Translator
ヘイヴンス・ノルマン　Norman HAVENS
Editor
関　裕志 SEKI Hiroshi
Assistant
星野博美 HOSHINO Hiromi
Special thanks to
週刊プレイボーイ(集英社)"Weekly PLAYBOY"
クレア(文藝春秋)"CREA"

ディ・マウアー/DIE MAUER

1991年10月5日 第1刷

著　者──橋口譲二
発行者──冨田耕作
発行所──情報センター出版局
　　　　東京都新宿区四谷2-1 四谷ビル 〒160
　　　　電話:03-3358-0231
　　　　振替:東京4-46236
印　刷──光村印刷株式会社
　　　　定価はカバーに表示してあります。
　　　　乱丁本・落丁本はお取替えいたします。
　　　　ISBN4-7958-0603-9

Text and Photographs:
©1991 by George Hashiguchi
Design:
©1991 by Takao Oshima
All rights reserved.
September 1991, first published by
JOHO Center Shuppan-Kyoku
2-1 Yotsuya, Shinjuku, Tokyo, Japan.
Printed in Japan by Mitsumura Printing Co., Ltd.

橋口譲二の本

ベルリン物語
壁の中の現代動物園・西ベルリン――むごくやさしいこの街で、自由を求め、自由に窒息する若者たち。彼らの明日へ向かう蘇生とは? 現代都市の予兆を描き切った記念碑的名作

まゆみさん物語
なんでも手に入ってしまう時代、たくさんあるように見える選択肢、けれどいま本当の「自由」って何? 満たされた現代ニッポンの空虚に出口を探した「ベルリン物語」姉妹篇

動物園
ベルリン・ロンドン・上海・モスクワ・ニューヨーク……世界14都市の動物園を巡り歩く。日常と非日常が微妙に入り交じった空間に、各々の人生の一瞬を読み取る。本格的写真集